Nocturnes

Paul Savoie

Translated by Jacques Lefebvre

BookLand press

Published by BookLand Press
15 Allstate Parkway, Suite 600, Markham, Ontario L3R 5B4
www.booklandpress.com

Printed and bound in Canada

Library and Archives Canada Cataloguing in Publication

Savoie, Paul, 1946-, author
Nocturnes / Paul Savoie; translated by Jacques Lefebvre.

Translation of: Bleu bémol.
At head of title: Winner of the Trillium Award for French-language poetry.
Issued in print and electronic formats.
ISBN 978-1-926956-88-6 (pbk.).--ISBN 978-1-926956-89-3 (epub).--
ISBN 978-1-926956-90-9 (pdf)

I. Lefebvre, Jacques, translator II. Savoie, Paul, 1946- . Bleu bémol. English. III. Title.

PS8587.A389B5313 2014 C841'.54 C2014-902092-9
C2014-902093-7

Canada Council for the Arts | Conseil des arts du Canada

ONTARIO ARTS COUNCIL
CONSEIL DES ARTS DE L'ONTARIO
an Ontario government agency
un organisme du gouvernement de l'Ontario

We acknowledge the financial support of the Government of Canada, through the National Translation Program for Book Publishing for our translation activities. We acknowledge the support of the Canada Council for the Arts, which last year invested $157 million to bring the arts to Canadians throughout the country. We acknowledge the support of the Ontario Arts Council (OAC), an agency of the Government of Ontario, which last year funded 1,681 individual artists and 1,125 organizations in 216 communities across Ontario for a total of $52.8 million.

In memory of my
grandmother Euphémie
who taught me the art
of weaving dreams

table of contents

an hour filled with ashes 7

blues in F minor 25

overthrow 35

blues in C minor 41

shattered glass 55

marble 61

blues in E minor 67

blues in E flat minor 75

an hour filled with ashes

I

the instant of clarity arrives
by refraction
upon the deviated lines of skin

of the insatiable mouth
the multiple beam attached to the sustaining wind
emanates unexpected flowers
the small storm awakens
a staccato of whispered words
against the eardrum

we must hang them in clever layers
the suddenly shaded mask
exorcising the animal
from the sensitive areas of the dream

the dawn is screaming
shattering glass
in the shadow of the heavens

II

uncertain stance
against the multiple images

exhaustion of body
reverse angle

delusional speech

everything shifts

III

the cloud streaks the skin
the signs in the margins of the frame
absorb the entire sky

the finger traces a thread
against the insatiable power
of the moon

IV

the face
in shadowy ripples
tattoos the skin
sheltered in white
chilled cities

you brush aside a lock of hair
you smile at the thought of endless waves
of shadow
and finally decide to end sideswiped

you're huddled at the bottom of your arch
a skewed tip
at the moment of the futile game
far from the shore

V

you stretch out your arms
in the form of a cross

that what you used as a receptacle
swirls inside you
a weak storm passing furiously
unlimited

you are born from your own rupturing
a sudden journey
in troubled skies

you still have the back of the map
the journey back
on the spinning board

a diagonal word
comes to shatter the void
you hear a faint sound of neighing
the wind with its frantic branches
builds ladders
for floating landscapes

a whisper softer than water
comes in glowing winding waterfall
to a shrivelled heart

when the jolt comes
you suffer
the opening of the wing

VI

the angled perception distorts the meaning

you turn the opposite way
towards what contradicts your reflexes

checkered cover
you are violent towards your own essence

the valve thinks it is a well
you breathe in

insects rave
stratify   haunting you
a crack
from the most painful
rescue

VII

you stay frozen by uncertainty

your mask protests
against your face
a ritual of the untamed world
that forces open your claws

we hear the animal scream
under the bushes

a door opens

the survivors take refuge
at the bottom of the den
prisoners of your sleep

VIII

the light makes you shine like makeup

your body is skin tight
the drum beats
like the finger that sometimes vibrates
on the saddest chord
the chord sustained by shredding

IX

wildflower
pushed by the silence of the subdued
you chisel kingdoms
among the imprints

mirrored
you gorge yourself
in small whirlwinds of malicious odours
and places of desolation

the resurrected turn to you
when collapsing
beg you
let your eyes darken them

you let the ground surge
and the staccatoed stem

X

a presence close to you
in front or behind you

almost at your side

a shadow maybe
projected in silhouette against the wall

you seem to be grazed
you measure the strength of abstract objects
their fragile appearance

you undo anything that has a hold on you

you slow down the pace
afraid to trigger the mechanism
its complex scaffolding
an irreversible action

what will no longer start
what probably will not
have an end

XI

you feel the tiny movement of objects
the panting in the enclosed space
the roar it causes in you
the mad dog
attracted by the smell of carnage

hand stained in blood

a sigh of someone agonizing

XII

a hand rests on your shoulder
you do not stop watching
straight ahead of you
in the opposite direction

you wait for the trigger

you see yourself appear against the current
an inescapable presence two steps away

in front or behind

ready to annihilate you

XIII

in successive trembling
by the rodent eye
dismembered body
under multiple reflections

fruit eroded
in successive tremors
of the troubled eye

satiated tongue
sated language

all feet and hands
swallow you whole

the body
from fall to fall
shifts the landscape

XIV

you slip as a snake
along my arms
the tender branch shudders
at your touch

the fruit in glittering clusters
hangs
ripened in the sun
under the shadow's peak

i bite, ferocious teeth
that split the pulp
under the sheets
and flickers a motley leaf
the beating heart

XV

we experience the hour of ashes
the one of swept dunes

the winds in caravan

cries of thirsty animals
in a sieve
against the surging horizons

a sandy parchment
for the distinguishing eye
that identifies the water drop
at the edge of the finger

XVI

when by interlocking fingers
the song of tenderness
clears the skin
all instruments in the world
we sound out the rustling and the end of season
through the open mouth
of those who will find love in one another

blues in F minor

you fall three times
from your chair
you roll on the ground
like those unloved
in his descent
into the shallows

sulphurous rain
along the walls
the sky
on each side of the window
clouds the eye

a woman caresses your neck
wipes the drool dripping from your chin

she sleeps at your side
despite the erratic movements
of your body against hers

such scorn spread in hiccups and spasms
on your cheek
between your teeth

jolts shaking the walls

curtains hang like spider webs
above your head

the woman stops
to wipe your forehead

she leaves the house
at the worst moment
and the deepest
silences

distress arises within
in oasis
croaking

the cactus masks the horizon
behind the sinuous sand

supplication to the burning bush
lit within you
on this fortieth day
of this fortieth desert

late late
in the mists of time

late
behind closed doors
of this hidden slab
far
so far
in the middle of a distant city

lost
lost from the only remains that you still have
from your reflection
on the glass

you scratch like a lost animal
the faint and unforgettable
imprint
against azure

even if your anger rises to your throat
this is not your anger
its bubbling
sends its cry
into the bowels

its serrated knife
cuts your umbilical cord

lifts your skull
to the dim light

the woman
arrives quietly
writes her name
on lips
of the dusty dunes

you turn your head
towards the sun
moping

you bellow
for hope

overthrow

dance on cobalt

you're the brush
the first trace along limestone and granite

hold me
to make me twirl on your devouring breath
eve to overthrow the dome of the eye

slice me with lightning blade
along the purplish cortex

dance on cobalt

you are the ground shaking
when the root pierces the canvas
the groove between what the world does not say
and what it leaves to emerge
the letter that the cracked sheet records
during its whirlwind
on the white and gray parchment
of the awakening

dance on cobalt

swallow me with hungry licking lips
digging into a strata weapon
burnished rays

of sighs
in bursts
your finger activates the season

the earth rumbles
the pulp of time vibrates
in your hands

dance on cobalt

this groove
that the dead leaf
carves on my skin

a lifeline
traced on your face
on the palm

the only sign of the longing
of the heart
during the frigid season

blues in C minor

i dodge among scattered objects
prisoners like me
from this mess
beneath the waves of thundering smoke

the floor   the ceiling   turn round and round
assault me
the darkroom eclipses me

silence roars a dreary slide
in outbursts that combine in the void
through resemblance with all the other missing

so many dead prowl
and darken the scene
locked in memory
in a shroud of colours
and murmurs

so many tender gestures
laid in wait
appetizers and tapas
drink filled glasses

i drink in large gulps that echo

eviscerated love
overlies the cloth
of shredded meat

everything is streaked
lines against stretched skin
elastic from a gesture
that the hand can no longer trigger

whirls wholly absorb
the gestures of love

i would cry tears into the folded mirrors
if there were not brown mists with no end
covering the lungs
greyish scars on the skin

frayed edges
of erasures
dwarfed
by the bluish ink
that can no longer
flow

the screams beat the tom-tom
in remembrance of intimate secrets
in a hut where i left you moan
felled like me
in this oasis of waiting

i expect when soothing music
intrudes between strides

all that exists here is round and stretched in time
rejection of your hand against mine
the daguerreotype that forms your lips upon
          my face
glued to the screen of a shattered dusk

i hear the murmur

music with no orchestra
foolishly leaves the heart to toss and turn
        in the shadow

a watermark on wicker
dust and divergence
of dream

we could barely hear the acoustics
of this darkened room

the strange whispering
marking time
memory adjusts to the compulsive beating

the heart does not know how the tempo beats
nor entrusts its chords to the wind

i would scream out loud
if the incestuous shrinking chords
ceased to tear away from my skin
if the constant moving of furniture
in the crushing of frames
flaying me alive

stop squeezing me with a breathless kiss
between two dry sips
a third one to swallow everything that cannot flow
a last one to punctuate
the overflowing that endlessly overfills
against suspended lips

stuck in their parallel chairs
ghosts exhale coils of melodic nights
astounded by dead zones
they barely recognize each other
in the twisting of in-between rays

i imbibe in a fragmented tempo

i dance their jig

i tear
into them

i shiver in yellowed ivory
trapped in flats
just before
or just after the hand
clinging desperately to the finger
stretches out to the most sustained notes
on the hard and infinitely long glissando

i splash of your smell
i am awash from head to toe
in your sweat
your head lands against my chest
emerging from one of my resurrections
          from the dead
more radiant in this annunciation
than the most crystalline transgressions

i dance on the track
that the notes
engraved in succession on the same bone
chiselled onto the whole

i empty myself in you
you evade me once more
with movement and disturbance

i escape from silhouette to silhouette
from large stain to a taint

i subscribe to every corner of life
that you spread on your linen rope
in unravelled cloth

i strike
in the wind

the piano beats against
the landscape

shattered glass

a soft word
slips between your lips
more muted even
than breath

you dare to smile
before my outstretched hand
you offer this caress between shattered glass

i hear the sound that rises in increments
even to the last gasp

ghosts are scattered
among ocher and clay
the table and chair dance
their arrangement

ceiling and floor
breaking the spin

the locking of our eyes
encrusted on the skin
in the greyed area
a bitter-sweet kiss

i lift a feverish hand
towards your shadow

you stop at the exact same moment, hanging
          suspended
in the void

marble

i offer this marble
it rolls rolls on the floor

limestone flooring
at your feet
clay road
remnants of dunes

you shape the scope
so that i walk
at a pace of eternity
near your cliff
where your drilling iris
pierces me
into my fault lines

i burst towards you
crumbled flame
deflected meteorite

love
in its fall
becomes smooth
a shift of a worm in the grooves of the floor
as noisy
as a gesture with the thumb against
          the screen of the night
as clever as the surface that draws the arch
until the end of the extension
to your palm

where i gravitate constantly
in my frantic race
to your lips

this marble rolls
by the corner of your eye

just at the height of the iris

flexible blade that cuts the eye in two

double-edged window
on the azure

the marble rolls
on each side of the abyss

i recognize you in the reflection

you tumble into me

blues in E minor

everything rings false
how can i live in such an arrangement
these three notes arranged so that
i lose my breath

i add a note
and a shrill is activated by the little finger
makes me teeter

back hunched
knees bent
i let myself be swept into the void
to the point of desolation
the farthest
from my being

water way
following the channel
carved by the ferocious machine

i arrive on a river bank
as a raft pulled by the current
is broken by the outcropping rock

laying on the floor
i ride on the safre
i gorge myself with anemone and columbine

the hand slips
to a softer note
an F sharp coupled to a C sharp
my ankles and wrists
untwist
vines play like reeds
their trestles
low and iridescent rays

i suck up the drop of water
that moistens my lips

my frantic fingers fuse
in simple notes
of the course that dazzles
that makes me gravitate to the source

i activate the shrill
i hold the note

i let the current invade me
my breath comes back

the horizon breaks
the falls free me

you place your hand in mine
the heart finally hears the beat of the day
the lips open

you reveal to me the name
you engrave me into the movement
the channel gives birth to the leaf
you pick me in the deadly season
all twisted by the end of the season
and even the waters roar

three notes that offer atonement
a note by watermark

an echo takes root

you prolong me within you
until the first chirp

the sun as migratory bird
leaden

an unknown season
settles within me

you hibernate under my skin

i remain
strangely rooted
sinuous flintlock
able to engage dusk

violet volcano
in its crystal strength
engraves signs of an outbreak on the skin

incandescent murmur
sails in between
tattooes my face

your lava flows
within me

blues in E flat minor

here are all my secrets
i spread them out before you
in small intervals between two notes
slightly rhythmic

there is
somewhere
a beat
at least a gasp
several phrases that you almost manage
        to pound out
from your fingertips
on the table made of oak

here
in the old dining room
of my grandmother
you will find the teacups
fine earthenware
the slightly chipped saucers
the teapot
coated in drawings
of lilacs

my grandmother offers cookies
she sips her tea
smokes her cigarette

the notes are linked
in a painfully slow rhythm
so slow
that it sounds like
what the fingers do
when working thread
to form the image
on the fabric

the picture emerges gradually
as if my grandmother
weaved a piece of music
from what she sees

sadness within gestures
like barely noticeable space
intervals between the notes
that punctuate the sentence

troubled words
that my throat painfully projects
to the screen of my lips

that which my mouth
weaves against your receiving eyes
as if i traced their extent
the barely shaped hieroglyphs
from the first pulsations of life

this furtive tam-tam
of my love for you
unable to satisfy a single accord
or single notes juxtaposed with infinity

love palimpsest that the voice provides
in double images
their flats in minor tones
the only offering
at the moment of confession

a gesture as strong as a concerto
as sweet
as the fabric that my grandmother feels
in her safe and patient hand

an old lady
leaning against the window
under the dazzling brilliance of summer rays
observes on the lawn
the three angels who observe her
from the collapsed fence

my grandmother turns to you
she stares into you
she smiles at you

the angels
invite us
to dance

we gravitate
towards the road

our accomplice fingers
weave
in the gap
in bits and pieces
that most closely resemble
love

we now look towards the window

we see the heavens dance

OTHER BOOKS BY THE AUTHOR

POETRY

L'incendiaire, co-authored with Dyane Léger. Montréal, Éditions du Marais, 2009.

CRAC, Ottawa, Éditions David, 2006. Prix Trillium.

Rivière et mer, Ottawa, Éditions L'Interligne, «BCF», 2006.

Fishing for Light, Windsor, Black Moss Press, 1998.

Racines d'eau (poèmes choisis), Montréal, Éditions du Noroît, 1998.

Oasis, Montréal, Éditions du Noroît, 1995.

Danse de l'oeuf, Ottawa, Éditions du Vermillon, 1994.

Shadowing, Windsor, Black Moss Press, 1993.

Amour flou, Toronto, Éditions du GREF, 1993.

Linked Alive (collectif), Montréal, Éditions Trois, 1990.

Bois brûlé, Saint-Boniface, Éditions du blé, 1989.

The Meaning of Gardens, Windsor, Black Moss Press, 1987.

Soleil et ripaille, Montréal, Éditions du Noroît, 1987.

Acrobats, Toronto, Aya Press, 1982.

La maison sans murs, Hull, Asticou, 1976.

Nahanni, Saint-Boniface, Éditions du blé, 1976.

Salamandre, Saint-Boniface, Éditions du blé, 1974.

PROSE

Dérapages, Ottawa, Éditions L'Interligne, 2012.

L'autre bout du monde, Ottawa, Éditions L'Interligne, 2009.

L'empire des rôdeurs, Ottawa, Éditions L'Interligne, 2004.

À tue-tête, Ottawa, Éditions L'Interligne, 1999.

Mains de père, Saint-Boniface, Éditions du blé, 1995.

Dead matter, Toronto, Crypt Editions, 1994.

Conversations dans l'Interzone, co-authored with Marguerite Andersen. Sudbury, Prise de parole, 1994.

Contes statiques et névrotiques, Montréal, Guérin, 1991.

À la façon d'un charpentier, Saint-Boniface, Éditions du blé, 1984.

ABOUT THE TRANSLATOR

Jacques Lefebvre is a bilingual French-English writer, editor, and translator. He was born in Quebec and grew up in northern Ontario. He has been translating literature, technical, and corporate documents from English to French and from French to English for many major Canadian, US, and international organizations for the last 11 years. His articles and short stories have been published in many magazines and newspapers in English and French. He is a member of the Writers' Union of Canada and the Literary Translators' Association of Canada.